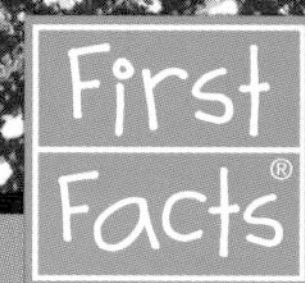

First Cookbooks

A BALLERINA COOKBOOK

Simple Recipes for Kids

by Sarah L. Schuette

CAPSTONE PRESS
a capstone imprint

First Facts is published by Capstone Press,
1710 Roe Crest Drive, North Mankato, Minnesota 56003.
www.capstonepub.com

Books published by Capstone Press are manufactured with paper containing at least 10 percent post-consumer waste.

Library of Congress Cataloging-in-Publication Data
Schuette, Sarah L., 1976–
A ballerina cookbook : simple recipes for kids / by Sarah L. Schuette.
p. cm. — (First facts. First cookbooks)
Includes bibliographical references and index.
Summary: "Provides instructions and step-by-step photos for making a variety of simple snacks and drinks with a ballet theme"—Provided by publisher.
ISBN 978-1-4296-7622-9 (library binding)
1. Snack foods—Juvenile literature. 2. Cooking—Juvenile literature. 3. Ballet—Juvenile literature. 4. Ballerinas—Juvenile literature. I. Title. II. Series.
TX740.S3256 2012
641.5'3—dc23 2011030310

Editorial Credits
Christine Peterson editor; Ashlee Suker, designer; Sarah Schuette, photo stylist; Marcy Morin, studio scheduler; Kathy McColley, production specialist

Photo Credits
All photos by Capstone Studio/ Karon Dubke except:
Shutterstock: Ambient Ideas (sequin texture), throughout, Ligak, 4 (right)

The author dedicates this book to Alindra K. Eilers.

Printed in the United States of America in North Mankato, Minnesota.
102011
006405CGS12

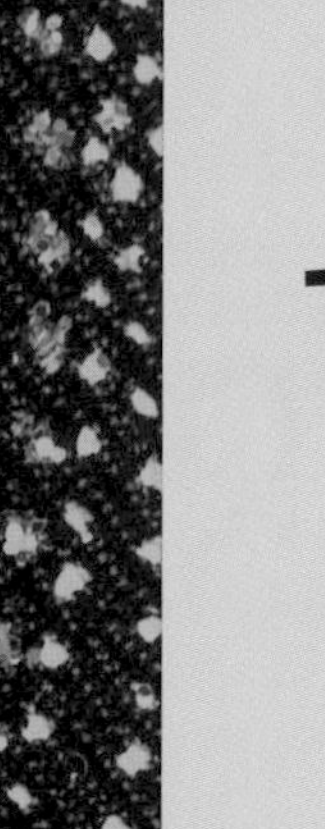

TABLE OF CONTENTS

BEAUTIFUL BALLERINAS

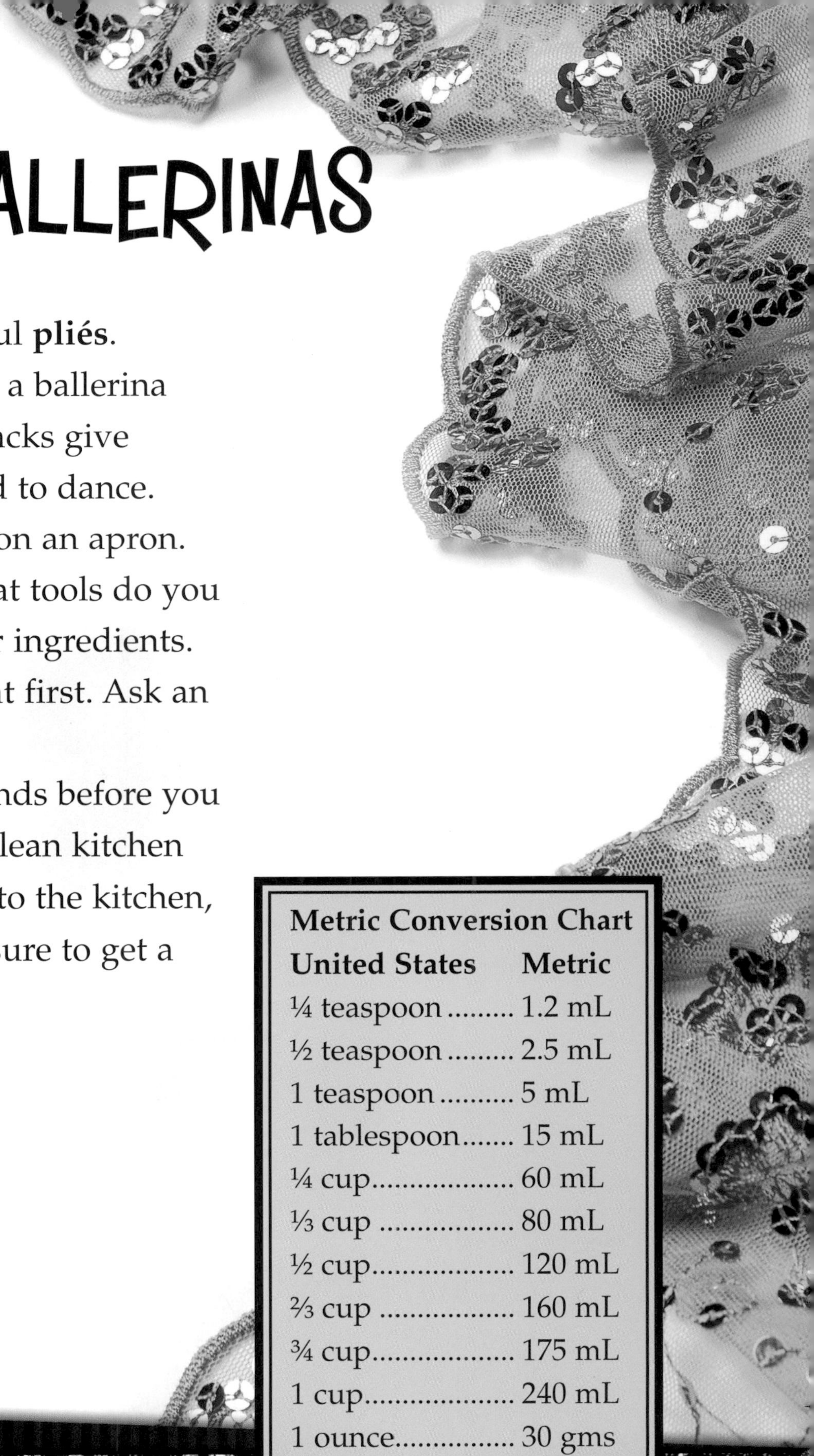

Spinning **pirouettes**. Graceful **pliés**. Dancing on **pointe** sure makes a ballerina hungry. Healthy meals and snacks give ballerinas the energy they need to dance.

Take off your **tutu**, and put on an apron. Read through each recipe. What tools do you need? Check the cupboards for ingredients. Every dancer needs a teacher at first. Ask an adult if you have questions.

Remember to wash your hands before you begin. And be sure to leave a clean kitchen when you finish. Now twirl into the kitchen, and get ready to cook. You're sure to get a standing **ovation**.

Metric Conversion Chart

United States	Metric
¼ teaspoon	1.2 mL
½ teaspoon	2.5 mL
1 teaspoon	5 mL
1 tablespoon	15 mL
¼ cup	60 mL
⅓ cup	80 mL
½ cup	120 mL
⅔ cup	160 mL
¾ cup	175 mL
1 cup	240 mL
1 ounce	30 gms

Tools

A ballerina makes sure her pointe shoes are tied just right before hitting the stage. You'll also need the right tools in the kitchen. Use this handy guide to track down the tools you need.

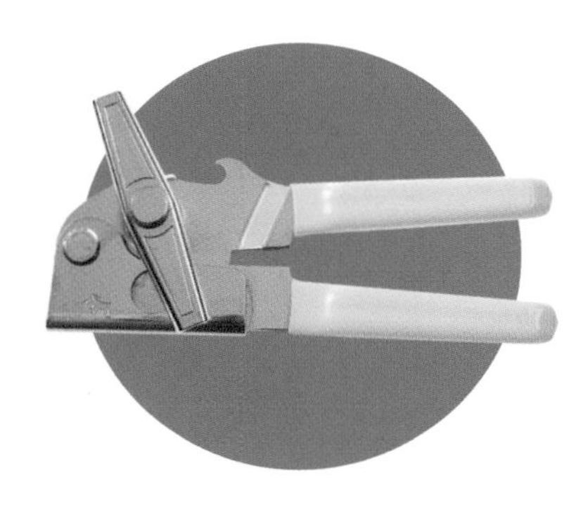

can opener—a tool used to open metal cans

cutting board—a wooden or plastic board used when slicing or chopping foods

dry-ingredient measuring cups—round cups with handles used for measuring dry ingredients

liquid measuring cup—a glass or plastic measuring cup with a spout for pouring

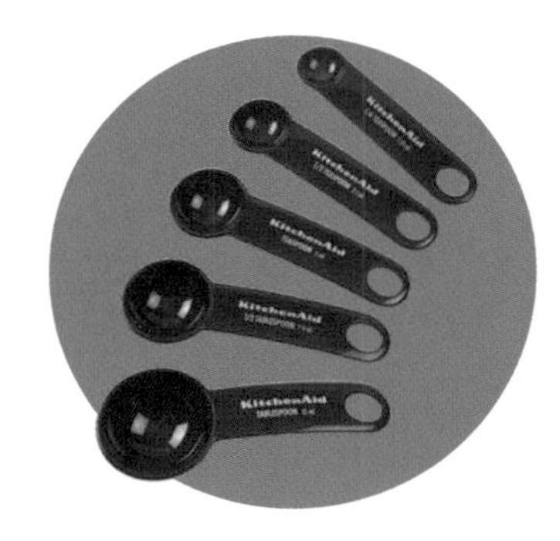

measuring spoons—spoons with small deep scoops used to measure both wet and dry ingredients

mixing bowl—a sturdy bowl used for mixing ingredients

pitcher—a container with an open top and a handle that is used to hold liquids

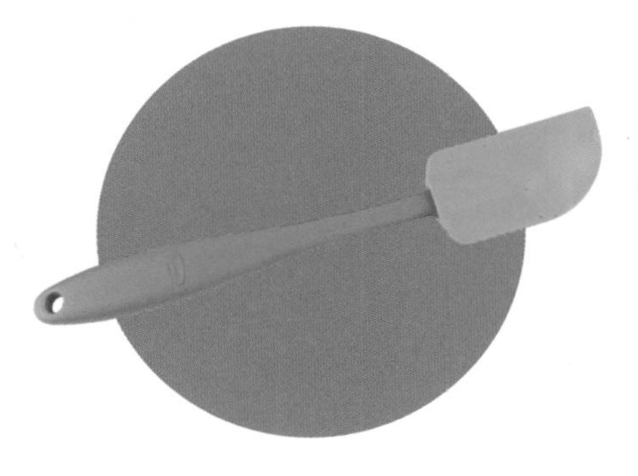

rubber scraper—a kitchen tool with a rubber paddle on one end

strainer—a bowl-shaped tool with holes in the sides and bottom used for draining liquid off food

wooden spoon—a tool made of wood with a handle and bowl-shaped end used to mix ingredients

TECHNIQUES

drain—to remove the liquid from something

measure—to take a specific amount of something

slice—to cut into thin pieces

spread—to cover a surface with something

sprinkle—to scatter something in small drops or bits

stir—to mix something by moving a spoon around in it

TUTU TOPPERS

Put on your fanciest tutu to eat these miniature fruit pizzas. They're perfect treats to eat on the way to your next lesson.

Serves 3

Ingredients:

- 3 graham cracker halves
- 2 tablespoons whipped fat-free cream cheese
- red food coloring
- sliced kiwis
- sliced strawberries
- blueberries

Tools:

- plate
- measuring spoons
- small mixing bowl
- spoon

1 Place graham crackers on a plate.

2 Measure cream cheese and put in small mixing bowl. Add red food coloring and stir until pink.

3 With a spoon, spread cream cheese on crackers.

4 Top each cracker with kiwis, strawberries, and blueberries.

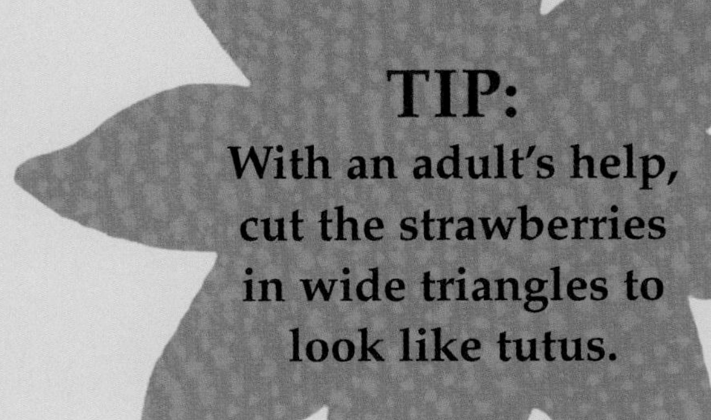

TIP:
With an adult's help, cut the strawberries in wide triangles to look like tutus.

PLIÉ POPPERS

Ballet is full of turns, twists, bends, and jumps. You'll want to jump for joy when popping these bites into your mouth.

Serves 6

Ingredients:

- 12 cherry or grape tomatoes
- ½ teaspoon Italian seasoning
- 1 tablespoon olive oil
- 6 butter or romaine lettuce leaves
- 12 small fresh mozzarella cheese balls

Tools:

- knife
- cutting board
- mixing bowl
- measuring spoons
- spoon
- plate

1 With an adult's help, cut tomatoes in half on a cutting board. Add tomatoes to mixing bowl.

2 Measure Italian seasoning and olive oil. Add to the bowl.

3 Gently mix ingredients together with a spoon.

4 Put a lettuce leaf on plate. With a spoon, fill lettuce with tomatoes and two mozzarella balls.

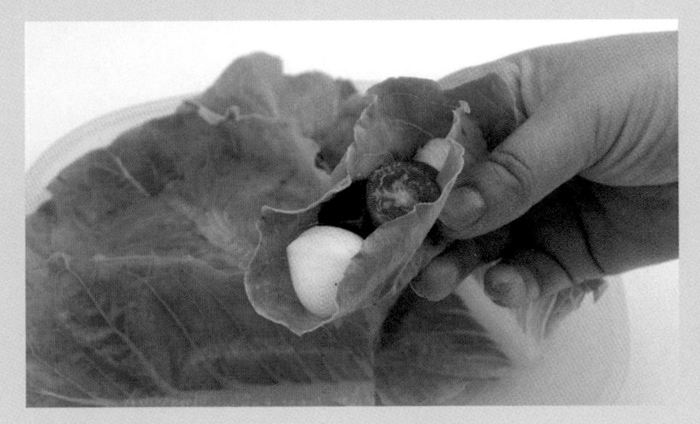

5 Roll lettuce around filling to eat. Use a toothpick to hold your roll together if you wish.

TIP:
Do you like spicy food? Just use chunks of pepper jack cheese instead of the mozzarella balls.

STAGE BITES

When you're dancing, don't think about the crowd watching you. Dream about these little bites instead. They will be waiting for you after the show.

Serves 3

Ingredients:

- 1 6-ounce can crabmeat
- ¼ cup fat-free sour cream
- ¼ cup fat-free mayonnaise
- dash Worcestershire sauce
- 1/8 cup shredded Monterey Jack cheese
- 3 slices whole grain bread
- chopped chives

Tools:

- can opener
- strainer
- mixing bowl
- dry-ingredient measuring cups
- spoon
- toaster
- plate
- crown-shaped cookie cutter

TIP:
Crabmeat not your favorite? Use mini shrimp or chicken instead.

1 Open crabmeat can, and drain liquid with a strainer. Add crabmeat to bowl.

2 Measure sour cream and mayonnaise. Add to bowl.

3 Add a dash of Worcestershire sauce to bowl. Measure and add shredded cheese to bowl. Mix with a spoon.

4 Toast bread and place on a plate. Use cookie cutter to cut a crown shape out of each slice of toast.

5 Spread crab mixture on each crown-shaped toast using a spoon.

6 Arrange chives around each crown to look like jewels.

TAKE A BOW BREAKFAST

Dancers know that eating a good breakfast gives them strength to do lifts and turns. Be sure to take a bow after making this healthy morning meal.

Makes 2 pancakes

Ingredients:
- 2 frozen pancakes
- 1 6-ounce container cottage cheese
- 1 fruit cup of peaches
- 6 raspberries
- ¼ cup granola

Tools:
- toaster
- plate
- dry-ingredient measuring cups
- spoon
- strainer

1 Heat pancakes in a toaster. Remove pancakes from toaster and place on a plate.

2 Measure cottage cheese. Using a spoon, spread ½ cup cottage cheese on each pancake.

3 Drain peaches with a strainer.

4 Top each pancake with peaches and raspberries.

5 Measure granola. Sprinkle half of the granola on each pancake.

TIP:
You can also use toaster waffles instead of pancakes. Or wrap the toppings in a tortilla for breakfast on the go.

RECITAL REFRESHERS

It's **recital** day! Celebrate your **performance** with this refreshing drink. It's sure to delight your guests and fellow dancers.

Serves 8

Ingredients:

- 6 ice cubes
- 6 cups cold water
- 2 cups cold apple juice
- 2 tablespoons powdered lemonade mix

Tools:

- pitcher
- liquid measuring cup
- measuring spoons
- wooden spoon

1 Add ice to pitcher.

2 Measure the cold water and pour into pitcher. Next measure and add apple juice.

3 Measure lemonade mix, and add to pitcher.

4 Stir with wooden spoon and serve.

NUTCRACKER SNACKER

Want sweet dreams? Before drifting away to the land of dancing snowflakes and sugar plum fairies, try this snack. It's a snack fit for the Nutcracker Prince.

Serves 2

Ingredients:

- ½ cup walnuts
- ½ cup almonds
- ¼ cup toasted pumpkin seeds
- ¼ cup sunflower seeds
- ¼ cup peanut butter chips
- ½ cup dried pineapple

Tools:

- dry-ingredient measuring cups
- mixing bowl
- spoon

1 Measure walnuts and almonds, and add to bowl.

2 Measure and add pumpkin seeds and sunflower seeds to bowl.

3 Next measure peanut butter chips and pineapple. Add to bowl.

4 Stir ingredients well with a spoon to mix.

PRIMA BALLERINAS

Prima ballerinas are the best of the best. Make your own prima ballerina using colorful fruit. This snack is sure to take center stage.

Serves 1

Ingredients:

- grapefruit
- small bunch of green grapes
- 2 blueberries
- 1 raspberry
- 2 cherries with stems
- apple slice

Tools:

- knife
- cutting board
- plate

1 Have an adult help you slice the grapefruit into rounds on a cutting board.

2 Place one slice of grapefruit on a plate. Use grapes to make hair.

3 Use blueberries for eyes.

4 Add a raspberry for a nose.

5 Next add the cherries as earrings.

6 Finish your prima ballerina by adding an apple slice for the mouth.

GLOSSARY

ingredient (in-GREE-dee-uhnt)—an item used to make something else

ovation (oh-VAY-shuhn)—a response with loud clapping cheering, and standing

performance (pur-FOR-muhnss)—the public presentation of a play, movie, piece of music, or dance

pirouette (peer-OOH-et)—a ballet move where the dancer spins on one leg with the other leg in one of many positions

plié (plee-EY)—a ballet movement in which the knees are bent and the back is straight

pointe (POINT)—a ballet move in which dancers are on the tips of their toes

recital (ri-SYE-tuhl)—a show where people sing, dance, or play a musical instrument for others

tutu (TOO-too)—a short ballet skirt made of several layers of stiff net

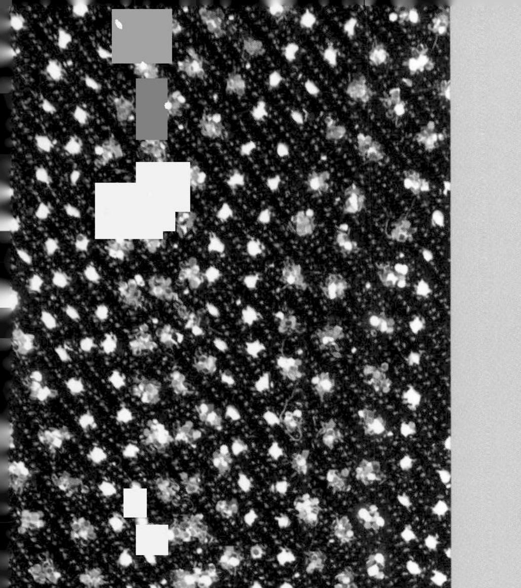

READ MORE

Alexander, Heather. *Easy Snacks From Around the World.* Easy Cookbooks for Kids. Berkeley Heights, N.J.: Enslow Publishers, 2011.

Schuette, Sarah L. *A Princess Cookbook: Simple Recipes for Kids.* First Cookbooks. Mankato, Minn.: Capstone Press, 2011.

Tuminelly, Nancy. *Super Simple Desserts: Easy No-Bake Recipes for Kids.* Super Simple Cooking. Edina, Minn.: ABDO Pub. Co., 2011.

INTERNET SITES

FactHound offers a safe, fun way to find Internet sites related to this book. All of the sites on FactHound have been researched by our staff.

Here's all you do:

Visit *www.facthound.com*

Type in this code: 9781429676229

INDEX